Urban Planner

Nel Yomtov

Published in the United States of America by Cherry Lake Publishing
Ann Arbor, Michigan
www.cherrylakepublishing.com

Content Adviser: Megan Masson-Minock, AICP, ENP and Associates, Ann Arbor, MI
Reading Adviser: Marla Conn, ReadAbility, Inc.

Photo Credits: ©Monkey Business Images/Shutterstock Images, cover, 1, 15; ©joebelanger/CanStockPhoto, 5; ©mediaphotos/iStockphoto, 6; ©Mosman Council/http://www.flickr.com/CC-BY-2.0, 9; ©Paul Matthew Photography/Shutterstock Images, 11; ©Goodluz/Shutterstock Images, 12; ©tovovan/Shutterstock Images, 17; ©Dorling Kindersley RF/Thinkstock, 18; ©Al-xVadinska/Shutterstock Images, 21; ©bowdenimages/iStockphoto, 21; ©Zastolskiy Victor/Shutterstock Images, 22; ©British Council Singapore/http://www.flickr.com/CC-BY-2.0, 25; ©Ohmega1982/Shutterstock Images, 27; ©Bernhard Richter/Shutterstock Images, 28

Library of Congress Cataloging-in-Publication Data

Yomtov, Nelson.
Urban planner / Nel Yomtov.
    pages cm. — (Cool STEAM careers)
 "Readers will learn what it takes to succeed as an urban planner. The book also explains the necessary educational steps,
useful character traits, and daily job tasks related to this career in the framework of the STEAM (Science, Technology,
Engineering, Art, and Math) movement. Photos, a glossary, and additional resources are included." Provided by
publisher.
Audience: Ages 8 - 12.
Audience: Grade 4 to 6.
Includes index.
ISBN 978-1-63362-009-4 (hardcover) — ISBN 978-1-63362-087-2 (pdf) — ISBN 978-1-63362-048-3 (pbk.) —
ISBN 978-1-63362-126-8 (ebook) 1. Vocational guidance—Juvenile literature. 2. City planning—Methodology—
Juvenile literature. I. Title.

HF5381.2.Y66 2015
307.1'216—dc23   2014026595

Cherry Lake Publishing would like to acknowledge the work of
The Partnership for 21st Century Skills. Please visit www.p21.org
for more information.

Printed in the United States of America
Corporate Graphics

ABOUT THE AUTHOR

Nel Yomtov is an award-winning author of nonfiction books and graphic novels for young readers.
He lives in the New York City area.

TABLE OF CONTENTS

STEAM is the acronym for Science, Technology, Engineering, Arts, and Mathematics. In this book, you will read about how each of these study areas is connected to a career in urban planning.

CHAPTER 1

PLANNING THE FUTURE

Adam and his mother were driving past the construction site of their town's new shopping center. Several buildings were partially completed. The land for the new roadways and parking lots was cleared and ready to be paved. Dozens of laborers were hard at work throughout the site.

"The new mall is going up fast!" Adam said.

"It sure is," said Adam's mother. "But did you know that the idea for the mall was proposed many years ago?"

"Why has it taken so long for it to be built?" Adam asked.

Careful planning is necessary as communities grow.

"That's because the development of a city is carefully worked out years in advance," she replied. "It takes lots of planning to make sure cities have places where people can live, work, and shop, as well as a good system of transportation."

"That sounds like a cool job," said Adam. "I'd love to be responsible for helping to plan the future of an entire city!"

City planning, also called urban planning, is an organized, inventive way to affect the future quality of

Urban planners consider a lot of information when making recommendations.

life in large cities, suburbs, small towns, and rural villages. The goal of urban planning is to create communities that are healthful, attractive, safe, and convenient for people to live, work, and play in.

The trained professionals who develop urban plans and programs are called urban planners. They gather information about a community's residents, its economy, and its environment. Urban planners also consider a city's transportation system, energy needs, housing supply, food resources, schools, shopping, and recreational activities.

After collecting and analyzing this information, urban planners develop ways that a city's government can improve its community. Planners determine if additional shopping facilities are needed and where they should be built. They might recommend new roads and improved public transit, new homes and schools, or even improved water lines and sewer systems. They may also recommend policy changes to allow **sustainable** energy programs or improved food access.

THINK ABOUT SCIENCE

In the early 2000s, the government of New York City and urban planners carefully reviewed scientific data about the effects of climate change. After analyzing the data, city officials decided to take steps to prevent future possible damage to the city. The city plans to build flood barriers and dune systems to combat rising sea levels. A plan for a mini elevated city, built above flood level, is also being considered. Creating workable, affordable designs for New York's flood prevention program will keep urban planners busy for years to come.

The scope of a planner's responsibilities varies from place to place and situation to situation. Some planners are responsible for specific, individual neighborhoods in a city or region. Other planners focus on many communities within a city or an entire region. Some planners work on projects that will be finished within a couple of years. Others develop plans for projects many years into the future.

Behind the scenes, planning is going on almost all the time in communities of all sizes. How do urban planners work, and what are the greatest challenges and rewards they experience?

Drawings, photos, and maps are all used by urban planners.

CHAPTER 2

GETTING IT DONE

Urban planning is about the future. Planners attempt to predict the future of a city or region and make **recommendations** that will help it thrive and meet the challenges that lie ahead. Planners often must look 5, 20, and even 50 years into the future to forecast the impact of current trends. Is a city's transportation system keeping up with the growing population? Is enough housing being built to meet increased demand? Will there be adequate places to shop or enough businesses to provide jobs? These are the difficult questions a city planner **grapples** with each day.

An urban planner does not make the final decision regarding which projects are undertaken. That decision is usually left in the hands of elected officials, such as a mayor and city council or people serving on a city's planning commission or planning board. After carefully studying the conditions of a city or region, the urban

Urban planners make recommendations about the number of housing units and kind of housing that should be built in a community.

Being able to work with others is an important skill for urban planners.

planner makes recommendations to city officials
that will hopefully ensure a brighter future for the
community. Where should the city allow growth or limit
development? How can the city attract business and grow
jobs? What new technologies can improve the city's
system of transportation? Urban planners investigate
the options and recommend the best solutions.

How do urban planners arrive at the right solution
that will affect a city 50 years in the future? They do it
by carefully studying the physical, social, and economic

conditions of a city. The physical environment includes its location, its climate, and its access to water and food. This environment also includes the type of soil, the amount of land covered by trees, the **watershed**, and the **topography**. The social environment includes the neighborhoods in which people live, the workplaces, and how people behave. The economic aspect of a community includes jobs, businesses, schools and universities, and cultural institutions.

THINK ABOUT TECHNOLOGY

As cities grow, more buildings, roads, subways, and bridges will need to be built. Energy use and traffic will increase. Today, planners create three-dimensional (3-D) computer representations of cities in which they can test various planning scenarios. The process allows planners to better determine the costs of projects. It also provides more accurate data to analyze and makes it easier to present visual concepts to city governments and the public for their approval.

Urban planners also gather information and seek advice from residents, government officials, and business executives. They might gain input from special interest groups, such as historic **preservation** organizations. Planners frequently consult with other professional experts, including architects, **engineers**, and environmental specialists.

Supplied with all of this information and data, planners develop strategies and solutions for solving problems and meeting the challenges of the future. They determine how their plans can be carried out, and, more importantly, how much their plans will cost. All of these findings are put into a document known as a **master plan**.

Meetings include sharing ideas, considering other's suggestions, and getting input from experts working in other fields.

THE MASTER PLAN

The master urban plan is a type of **blueprint** for the growth and development of a community. It usually includes many reports, articles, charts, graphs, and computer-generated maps. A master plan can be the result of anywhere from weeks to months—or even years—of research. Among other issues, a typical master plan addresses:

- Land use. This part of the plan shows how the land in a community will be used in the future. For example, will there be designated **mixed-use** areas,

Graphics like this help give urban planners a look at waterways, roads, and open spaces in a community.

which combine residential, **commercial**, and cultural places in the same development?

- Transportation and traffic. How will people and goods move from one part of the community to another? This step looks at a city's roads, subways, bicycle and walking paths, rivers, and other means of transportation.

- Housing. How much housing will be needed for the future? What types of housing will be required? This part of the plan looks at current housing conditions

This type of illustration may be used by an urban planner to help share ideas with community officials.

and offers suggestions to meet future population and economic trends.

- Environmental issues. This aspect of the plan focuses on two issues: how the city can preserve its natural environment and how the city's development will affect the environment. Will pollution from newly created factories or increased automobile traffic harm the environment and people's health?

- **Infrastructure**. The infrastructure of a city includes its roads, bridges, water supply, power lines, schools, and many other services and facilities that keep the city running.

Urban planners develop a master plan with continued input and advice from city officials, politicians, businesspeople, and the public. Part of an urban planner's job is to educate people on the research that was done to develop the details of the plan.

THINK ABOUT ENGINEERING

Urban planners often work with a wide variety of other professional experts. Among them are civil engineers, the people who design and oversee construction projects of all kinds. Civil engineers focus on the projects themselves, while planners are responsible for determining which projects are necessary and how they fit into the overall master urban plan. A basic understanding of engineering principles can be a handy tool for all urban planners.

WORKING WITH OTHERS

One of the most critical parts of a city planner's job is to get support and money to carry out a program. Most of the money comes from governments. Governments use tax money collected from the public.

Urban planners meet with government officials and the public during the entire planning process. They explain their ideas and get **feedback** from the people who will be affected by their proposed projects. This helps ensure the ideas are correct for the entire community. Planners often provide the community with maps, photos, and designs

Urban planners must be comfortable speaking in front of groups.

that explain their concepts. Planners revise or **abandon** their projects if the public believes they are too expensive or do not adequately serve the best interests of the community.

Gaining political and public support for a master plan can be tricky—and frustrating—for the urban planner. Elected government officials may come and go during the planning process. This can result in shifting attitudes and policies toward the planner's recommendations. Extended debate or opposition from the public can delay decisions

Scale models like this help an urban planner share an idea.

and actions on the plan. Smart urban planners get all interested parties involved in the planning process early and often. They gather valuable feedback and use it to improve their proposals.

About 65 percent of urban and regional planners work in local government. Others work for state and federal governments. Roughly 25 percent of urban planners work for architectural and engineering firms, management and scientific firms, and nonprofit organizations.

A typical day for an urban planner usually includes office meetings and presentations. Conducting research and gathering data is also part of the normal workday. Planners use a variety of cutting-edge technologies, including a geographic information system, or GIS. This computer system allows planners to collect, store, and manage all types of geographical data.

Other tools include financial spreadsheets, such as Excel, and demographic databases, which include statistics about residents' ages, languages, ethnicities, and much more.

THINK ABOUT ART

While most planners are not skilled artists, having the ability to work with drawings, photographs, and maps is useful for every planner. Use of 3-D software like SketchUp or Photoshop lets planners give a visual picture of what an area would look like if planned changes occurred. While a skyscraper might be visually appealing, SketchUp can also show how the shadow of the skyscraper would affect nearby houses.

CHAPTER 5

YOUR CAREER AS AN URBAN PLANNER

Urban planners require a mix of skills and the right education to plan the future of Earth's cities. Planners need strong communication skills. They must frequently write reports and deliver oral presentations. They speak regularly with city officials, residents, and experts in many fields. Therefore, the ability to convey information clearly and accurately to a diverse group of people is essential.

Urban planners need to have strong research skills. Planners sift through market research studies, polls,

Weekly nighttime meetings are often required to share information with the public and elected officials.

environmental impact studies, and all types of databases to gather information vital to the planning process. Once they collect this information, planners must accurately analyze it. Then they must consider all planning options to create appropriate recommendations and action steps.

An ability to handle basic math concepts such as figuring percentages and ratios and solving simple equations is required for urban planners. These skills are especially handy when explaining tables, charts, and graphs to city officials and the public.

Most planners are capable of using computer-based technologies, such as Global Positioning Systems and GIS. Many urban planners use software that creates **models** to predict the impact of new structures and services on people and the environment.

The right education will put you on the productive path toward being an urban planner. About 62 percent of planners hold a master's degree in planning. People usually enter master's degree programs in planning with many different kinds of bachelor's degrees. Some planners earn their undergraduate degree in sociology, economics, architecture, engineering, or a host of other disciplines. Many master's programs offer specialty degrees, including transportation planning, urban design, and environmental planning.

The job outlook for urban and regional planners looks bright. The U.S. Bureau of Labor and Statistics reports that employment is projected to grow 10 percent by the year 2022. In May 2012, the median annual wage

Understanding computer software and the models it creates is important for an urban planner.

*Recommendations made by an urban planner will
impact the lives of others for many years to come.*

for planners was about $65,000. The median salary is the
wage that half the workers earn more than and half earn
less than. The highest salaries are offered in the private
sector, where planners often work in architectural and
engineering firms.

The demand for well-educated, experienced urban
planners will continue throughout the 21st century. Planners
will be needed to address the impact of population growth,
environmental concerns, and deteriorating infrastructure.
Municipalities will turn to planners to deal with housing

needs, improved transportation systems, job growth, and historic preservation.

Urban planning is an exciting and challenging career. Planners shape communities for decades to come and have a meaningful impact on people's quality of life. They face new challenges and opportunities each day.

If creating plans to help cities and people grow and prosper appeals to you, perhaps urban planning is in *your* future. Are you up to the challenge?

THINK ABOUT MATH

If urban planning is in your future, take as many math courses as your school offers. Learn how to use spreadsheets, such as Excel, which will teach you how to organize numbers as a table or chart. In college, you should pursue courses in higher mathematics, including calculus and trigonometry. Planners also use statistics to understand the characteristics of a community's residents, such as their age, income level, and the quality of their housing.

THINK ABOUT IT

Why is urban planning important to the future development of a community or city? See if you can come up with a list of at least five problems that communities would have without the work of an urban planner.

Describe a master urban plan. What are the most important issues addressed by a master plan? Visit your local government offices and see if someone there can show you a master plan.

Read chapters 2 and 5 again. How do urban planners use technology and mathematics to perform their jobs?

LEARN MORE

FURTHER READING

Dyer, Hadley. *Watch This Space: Designing, Defending and Sharing Public Spaces.* Toronto: Kids Can Press, 2010.

Jakab, Cheryl. *Sustainable Cities.* Mankato, MN: Smart Apple Media, 2010.

Spilsbury, Richard. *Towns and Cities.* Chicago: Heinemann Library, 2013.

Yomtov, Nel. *Transportation Planner.* Ann Arbor, MI: Cherry Lake Publishing, 2013.

WEB SITES

American Planning Association—Kids and Community
www.planning.org/kidsandcommunity
Get the facts on transportation planning, environmental planning, and urban design, plus lots more, from the United States' leading professional planning organization.

How Stuff Works—How Urban Planning Works
http://science.howstuffworks.com/environmental/green-science/urban-planning.htm
Learn about the history of urban planning, how urban planning works, and what a master urban plan looks like.

GLOSSARY

abandon (uh-BAN-duhn) to give up

blueprint (BLOO-print) a detailed plan of action

commercial (kuh-MUR-shuhl) of or having to do with making money or buying and selling things

engineers (en-juh-NEERZ) people who are specially trained to design and build large machines or structures, such as bridges and tunnels

feedback (FEED-bak) written or spoken reactions to something that is being done

grapples (GRAP-uhlz) tries to figure out or deal with something

infrastructure (IN-fruh-struk-chur) the basic facilities necessary for a community to function, including roads, bridges, water pipes, and power lines

master plan (MAS-tur PLAN) a comprehensive long-term strategy

mixed-use (MIKST-use) combining residential and commercial development

models (MAH-dulz) something built as an example of something larger, to see how it will work or look

preservation (prez-ur-VAY-shuhn) keeping alive or in existence; keeping safe from harm or injury

recommendations (rek-uh-men-DAY-shunz) suggestions or proposals that offer the best course of action

sustainable (suh-STAY-nuh-buhl) done in a way that can be continued and that doesn't use up natural resources

topography (tuh-PAH-gruh-fee) the physical features of an area

watershed (WAW-tur-shed) a land area that drains into a river or lake

INDEX